contents • contents

tallest

shortest

This doll is tallest.

This doll is shortest.

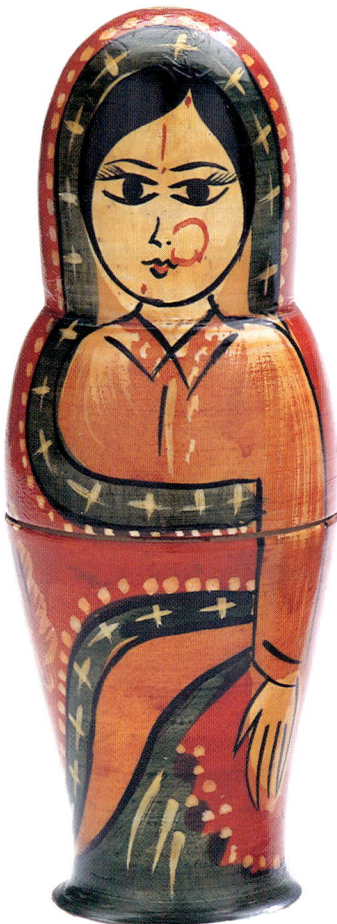

Which is tallest?

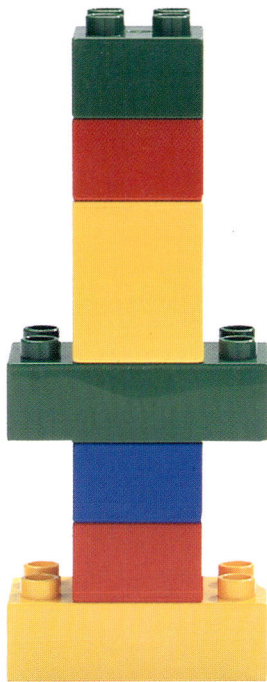

1   2   3   4

To do:
Copy the towers above.
Now draw some more
bricks on number 1
to make it the tallest.

longest

shortest

This is shortest.

This is longest.

Which is longest?
Which is shortest?

To do:
Find some pens and pencils. Line them up. Put the longest at the top. Put the shortest at the bottom.

Sometimes you need to know how long or how tall something is.

You can measure with anything.

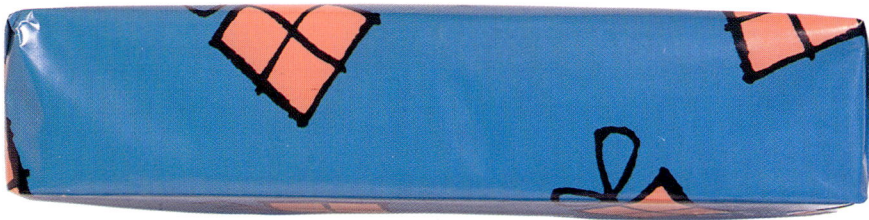

Measure with the same thing.
This present is 9 pasta tubes long.

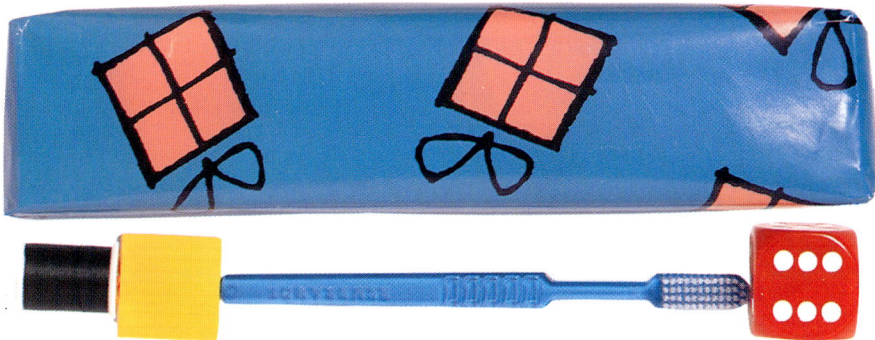

It is hard to measure well with different things.

How many boxes tall?

To do:
Use your open hand to measure with.
How many hands long is your table?
How many hands tall is your table?

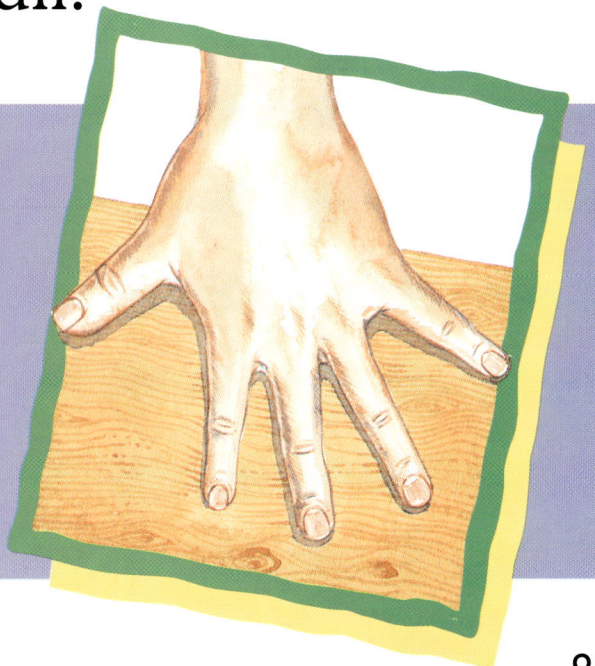

It is best if everyone uses the same thing to measure.
We measure in centimetres (cm for short) and metres (m for short).
100 centimetres = 1 metre.

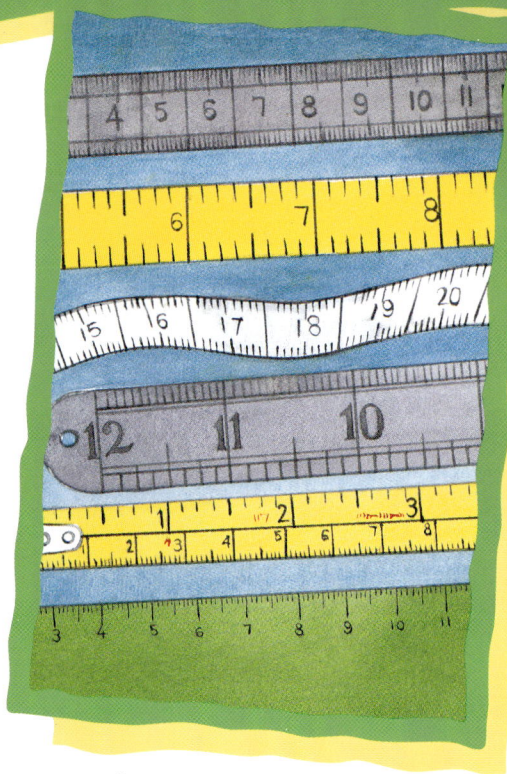

Kieran is 132 cm tall.

He is 59 cm around.

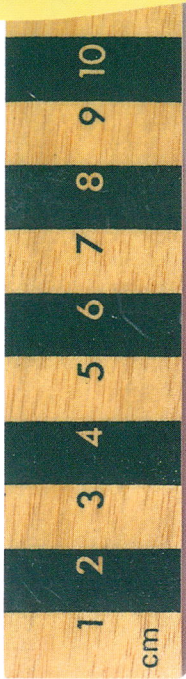

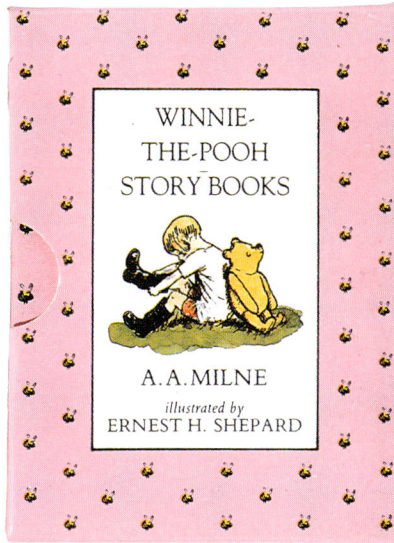

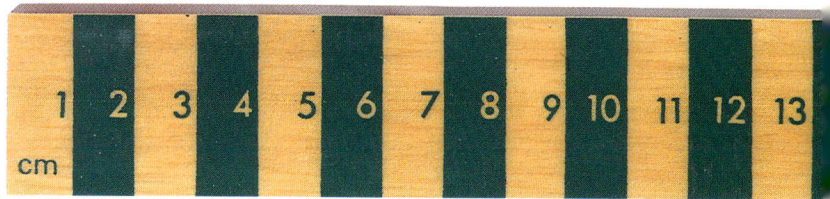

How many
cm long?
How many cm wide?

To do:
Estimate (guess) how
many cm long your
foot is.
Measure it.
Estimate (guess) how
many cm it is around
your head.
Measure it.

We use scales to
weigh things.
They tell us
which is heaviest.
The heaviest thing
makes the scales go down.

The dinosaur is heavier.
The ball is lighter.

What is lighter?

To do:
What is lighter
than a bed?
What is heavier
than a ball?

We weigh things in grams (g for short) and kilograms (kg for short). 1000 grams = 1 kilogram.

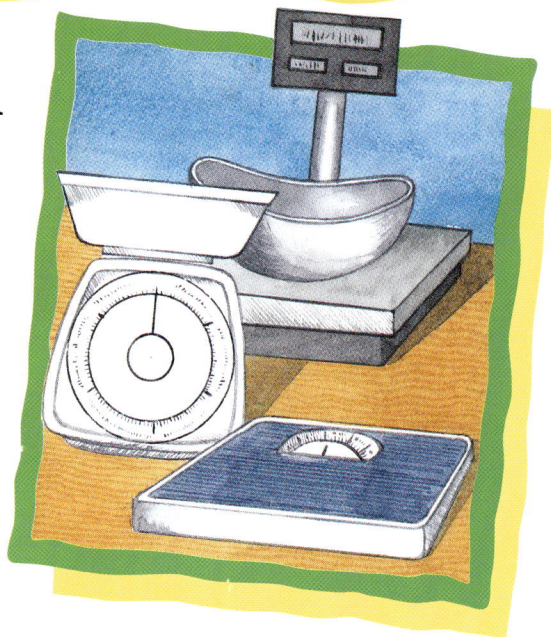

These sweets weigh 1 kilogram.

1 kg

1 kg

These potatoes weigh 1 kilogram.

How much does this flour weigh?

To do:
Does the packet of biscuits weigh more than the bag of sugar?

PURE CANE
SUGAR
1 kg

DIGESTIVE
BISCUITS

The jug holds more juice than the glass. We say that the capacity of the jug is greater than the capacity of the glass.

6 glasses of juice will fill this jug. The capacity is the amount of juice the jug will hold.

We measure liquid capacity in millilitres (ml for short) and litres (l for short).

To do:
Estimate (guess) which will hold the most water: a cup or a bowl.

Fill a cup and bowl with water to see if you were right.

Clocks measure time in minutes and hours.
The long hand points to the 12 (to show o'clock).
The short hand points to the 8 (to show the hour).

This clock shows 8 o'clock.

what time? • what time?

One clock shows a different time
from all the others.
What time does it show?
What time do the other clocks show?

To do:
What time is it?

19

Digital clocks do not have hands. They show the time just using numbers. This clock shows 8 o'clock. The number before : shows the hour. The number after : shows the minutes. **:00** shows o'clock.

10 o'clock.

What time is it?

To do:
Write these times down
as digital time.

We measure time in hours, days, weeks, months and years.

24 hours = 1 day. 7 days = 1 week.
52 weeks = 1 year. 12 months = 1 year.

6 years old today.

How old will this girl be
in 12 months time?

To do:
When is your birthday?
How many months old
are you?

DECEMBER

			Joe's Birthday		
3	4	5	6	7	1	2
10	11	12	13	14	8	9
17	18	19	20	21	15	16
24/31	25	26	27	28	22	23
					29	30

answers

index